# Ari's Wild Video Idea

Story by Cameron Macintosh
Illustrations by Monika Róża Wiśniewska

## Contents

## Chapter 1

# An Interesting Competition

"Ari!" called Mum. "It's time to get up. You're going to be late for school!"

Ari yawned and looked at his clock. It was 8:45 am, which gave him only fifteen minutes to get dressed and have breakfast. Then he would have to log on to his computer to start school for the day.

As Ari got dressed, he looked out through his bedroom window. The sun was already beating down on the wheat growing on his family's farm.

Ari made it to the computer just in time. His older brother, Luke, had already logged on to his own lesson at the other end of the room.

Ari could see his classmates on the screen. They all lived on remote farms like his.

"I have some interesting news today," said his teacher, Ms Tomasi. "I know how much you all love digital devices. We're going to be using them for our next project!"

The class was keen to hear more.

"I've just heard about a video-making competition for school students," said Ms Tomasi. "The judges want you to use the camera on a phone or tablet to make a short video about your life. Your video can show something special about your home, or hometown, so other students can see how you live."

Everyone was excited about the competition – except for Ari. He looked around the living room, and out the window at the fields of wheat.

*I don't think I can make a very interesting video about my home*, he thought to himself.

Ari's thoughts were interrupted by his classmate Will, who was loudly telling the class that he already had lots of exciting ideas for his video. "I'll show myself riding on the BMX track on our farm," Will said. "And then I'll show myself with Dad, sailing our boat on the bay!"

*Will's life is much more exciting than mine,* thought Ari, with a sigh. *I can't compete with a BMX track and a sailboat.*

## Chapter 2

# A Walk Around the Farm

After school, Ari sat at his desk and thought about the competition. It sounded fun, but he still didn't think his family's farm was interesting enough to show in a video.

Ari decided to go for a walk, hoping to find something he could film. He wandered around the farm, looking at the farm animals, the buildings and the equipment his parents used to cut the wheat they grew.

"No," he sighed. "There's nothing interesting here at all."

The next morning, Ms Tomasi asked the class if anyone had come up with ideas for their videos.

Will told the class he had already started work on his video. "My sister Mia filmed me riding my BMX around our track. I did some really cool jumps. I can't wait to show you all!"

Lana had started work on a video, too. “My video shows me helping Dad clean the plane he uses for his job as a flying vet,” she told the class.

Even Sami, who usually didn’t say much in class, was excited about filming the huge windmill her parents were building on their sugar cane farm.

At the end of the class, Ms Tomasi asked Ari to stay online after the other students had left.

"Is everything all right, Ari?" she asked. "You don't seem very keen about the competition."

"I am keen," Ari replied, "but I can't think of anything interesting to film around here."

"I think a lot of people would find your farm interesting, especially people who live in big cities," replied Ms Tomasi. "This afternoon, I'd like you to walk around your farm and take photos of all the things you wouldn't find in a big city."

Ari wasn't sure how that would help, but he agreed to give it a try.

Chapter 3

# Some Helpful Visitors

Shortly after logging off, Ari went outside. He borrowed his brother Luke's phone and wandered around the farm, taking photos of all the animals, equipment and farm buildings.

When he went back inside, he sat down and looked at each photo. *No one in the city would find this farm interesting*, he thought.

Just as Ari was about to turn the phone off, he noticed something unusual in the photo of the barn. On top of it, he could see an eagle, stretching out its wings.

Ari went back and looked more closely at the other photos.

Behind the tractor, he saw a pair of rabbits. In another photo, a flock of ducks was flying over the shed. The ducks and rabbits were nothing unusual to him, but Ari began to wonder if city people might find them interesting.

*Maybe I can make a video about the wild animals that visit our farm*, he thought.

## Chapter 4

# Filming with Luke

All through the weekend, Ari and Luke walked around the farm with Luke's phone, filming the animal visitors.

On Sunday, they got up early to make sure they filmed the birds in the trees.

Later that day, Ari found a lizard sunbathing on a rock. While Luke filmed him with the lizard, Ari shared a story about a time he had mistaken this kind of lizard for a snake. He had jumped backwards in fright and had almost fallen over!

That evening, with Luke's help, Ari used the footage on the phone to make a five-minute video.

His video showed all sorts of creatures – ducks, lizards, birds, rabbits and more.

On Monday, Ari shared his video with the class. Everyone enjoyed it, even Will. They all laughed when they heard the story about the lizard.

By the end of the class, Ari was very excited about entering his video into the competition.

Chapter 5

# One More Award

A few weeks later, Ms Tomasi told the class that the judges had chosen the winners of the video-making competition. They all logged on to watch the presentation and listen to the judges talk about the entries.

"More than 300 students sent in videos," said one of the judges. "We were impressed by the quality of them all. But unfortunately, not everyone can win a prize."

"Third place goes to Danny West, for his video about life on a wind farm," said the judge. "Well done, Danny!"

Another judge took over. "Second place goes to Eva Lonsdale, for her video about living in a houseboat," she said.

"And, in first place," said the last judge, "is Will Nolan, whose very active lifestyle impressed us all. Congratulations, Will!"

Ari was disappointed that he hadn't won a prize, but he was proud that Will had done so well.

Just as Ari was about to log off, one of the judges said, "Finally, we have one more award. This award is for the video that the students voted as their favourite. The award goes to ... Ari Baros!"

"Well done, Ari," said Ms Tomasi, smiling. "See – your home is much more interesting than you think it is!"